Turning

Turning

Poems of Migration and Identity

Tony Kendrew

PILEATED PRESS

2020

Cover layout and design:
Michael Rickard

Kendrew, Anthony G.
Turning
Poems of Migration and Identity

Library of Congress Control Number: 2020909220
ISBN 978-0-9626456-1-7

Pileated Press
4751 Feliz Creek Road
Hopland, CA 95449

First Printing 2020

In gratitude to the real and imaginary beings
who inspired these poems,
and to the people and the beauty of Wales.

Contents

Introduction

The Welsh have a word for it, that discomfort familiar to people the world over, the deep longing to return home: *hiraeth*. This longing is not just an affliction of wanderers, refugees and the displaced; *hiraeth* can visit us in the comfort of our own living rooms. It is universal enough to point to something about the nature of the human condition. The poems in this book approach and explore this feeling from many angles, though they are in English, so the word *hiraeth* does not appear.

Turning is a collection of poems that reflects on the urge to migrate and explore, and how that urge relates to a sense of place and belonging. The idea to use an exploration of my own background and origins as the anchor for the *Turning* poems arose during the first year of my Creative Writing MA at Trinity Saint David, Lampeter, Wales. I wanted to write about how this expansive urge was expressed in my own family and life.

The poems go in two directions, one towards the history of the Welsh side of my family, the other towards the nature of nationality and diaspora in general. A final reflection touches on the nature of the longing for home and belonging.

If we think of this collection of poems in musical terms as a suite of variations on a theme, the first poem is the overture, a fanfare to youth's urge to explore. The movements that follow are chronologically arranged, allowing the story of awakening to my ancestry to be told, with historical reconstructions pinned to time and place. More general reflections are interspersed undated.

Explicitly or implicitly, the poems explore the need to break away from the confines of family, from poverty and nutritional inadequacies, or from an unsuitable climate, and the need to find adventure, or a mate, to open new land and explore, whether for scientific or geographical knowledge or commercial gain. They also hint at something deeper and unconscious, which could call genetic determinism, a biological need to spread our seed to ensure genetic diversity.

We are held back from this outward movement by our ties to family and ancestry, to land, landscape and climate, to patterns of behavior, rituals, habits, religions and language. If and when we return, we face a second break with the past, the adoption of a new identity, the possibility of disillusionment, and a realization of the maturity of these discoveries.

The poems that tell stories of members of the Welsh side of my family are poetic fantasies, not intended to be accurate character portraits or records of events. They are attempts to capture some of the characteristics of Welshness with illustrations of the joys and tragedies of family and diaspora. As the poems took shape I had the impression of getting to know these people for the first time, though their traits and idiosyncrasies were found in my own behavior, rather than in stories and reports about them.

The collection is ultimately not about Welshness in particular. It ends by going beyond attributes, beyond nationality and identity, and is less about finding an external place than rediscovering an internal state of being.

Hiraeth is reframed as the longing for the content-ment of the home within, in whatever psychological or spiritual or religious terms we wish to express it, rather than the nostalgia of the home on the hill. While there may always be a welcome in the hillside, home is where the heart is. There are no roots like the roots in the ground of the present moment.

Hopland, California, May 2020

New World

so he goes forth
almost a man
a year or two past gangly
striding out the kitchen door
armed with oiled steel
to break ground
make something his own
claiming other for mine
stepping beyond the anonymity
of his enslavement to youth
double digging
the first earth
taming a world
where sedges mark the boundaries
of the virgin territory
drawn on his chart
the extent of it
the draining of the swamp

he stands
bare-chested
well-fleshed about the bones
sweating
his muscles shake
at every strike
the slide of tines in earth
the crunch of tools through rust and grit
the tower of his body
raising high the weapon
hear him roar the height of his anger

watch him turn to blaze his eyes
hear him shout his triumph

see the design of him
the pivotal length of arm
the heave of shoulders eclipsing sun
the arc of the tool
the structure of the hand
the fullness of its growth
gripping the sword
gloves, helmet, boots

imperative of survival
imperative of conquest
a simple equation
they have it
we need it

so he plunges his sword
into the skull of the land
makes the earth his blood
the blood his nourishment

another cave
another water source
another valley
seen from a ridge
moving north
to softer lands
towards the end of day
expanding west

to another shore
where waves break
on a tide of cities
echoing with the sound of rape
the cry of babies

shall we place our finger on the wound
staunch the flow
draw the line
drown the babies
turn the ships around
at Hastings, Plymouth, Botany Bay?

or wait
for the next proud planet
to capitulate
to the same ambition
the same disregard for those who call it home
the slash and burn of ruthlessness
indifference to the boot-crushed weeds
on the road's verge
the discarded cigarettes
the empty cans of beer

until
a few miles behind
a few centuries later
when the flesh is consumed
when the vultures have moved on
and the sun has bleached the bones
hierarchy follows youth

into the ashes
to make amends
restore the wasteland
glean scrap from the battlefield
clean the wells

they look around, they build
clay, sticks, stones, mortar
replace the green of mildew
with the spring of grain
with the stirring
of the first shoots of conscience
reviving the memory
of the consequences of action
of history repeating itself
of a rationale for pillage
of justifications for appropriation
documents, treaties, titles,
fences, maps
homelands, reservations
prison camps

how long till we forget?
feet dancing in the firelight
again
the children's cries
flushing the heron
from the river bank

Tregaron, 1854

I have a grand time
with the boys on market days
and there's nothing like
the smile of neighbors
after chapel. Then

walking home together
the sun on the blackthorn
and the land shining
Beca trying to trip me
laughing her bonnet off
her black hair flying.

But how quickly
the sentiment turns to dudgeon
the silence of the broth to tedium
the knock of spoon on bowl
signaling from dissenting walls.

And at the fall of night
no candle breaks the darkness
that seals this farmhouse
closes on the click of door latch
in and out forever to the fold.

Betsi Davis did it
just walked away and she a girl
left Bala to her sisters
joined the drovers' walk to London
one less mouth to feed.

I could leave these walls behind
these fields this clinging mud
the chapel rising from the grass
this ancient farm
Cymraeg.*

---

* Betsi Davis, born Elizabeth Cadwaladr, left home at the age of fourteen
and became well-known later in life when she joined Florence Nightingale
in the Crimea. Cymraeg is the Welsh language.

18

There was a Curious Welshman

◡ After John Keats' *A Song About Myself: There Was a Naughty Boy, I & IV*

There was a curious Welshman
And a curious man was he
He would not stay at home
And could not settled be –
So he put
In his knapsack
A book
Full of hymns
A family photograph
Curled at the rims
A clean shirt
Breeches
And a Monmouth cap
For a nice warm nap
A hair brush
Tooth ditto
And new socks –
For old ones
Would split-O!
He set off
With his knapsack
Tight on his back
And followed his dreams
To the West
To the West
And followed his dreams
To the West.

There was a curious Welshman
And a curious man was he
He sailed to California
The gold for to see –
There he found
That the ground
Was as poor
That a law
Was as tough
That enough
Was as rare
That a bear
Was as brown
That a clown
Was as sad
That naughty
Was as bad
And a hymn
Was as tuneful
As in Wales –
So he stood in his boots
And he wondered
He wondered
He stood in his boots
And he wondered.

Pant y Hirion, 1876

Is there a way to bridge the years
now the forest has darkened the mountain
and covered the mineshafts
now a wrought-iron gate
makes us back up
half way to the road?

The view is much the same
northwest down the Rheidol
to Aberystwyth.
Somebody built right here
for that view –
must have loved the summer sunsets
over the Lleyn.

What made you leave this place?
Send your wife to her mother
with your children?
And what did you tell them
when you left for Liverpool?
God be with you?
Look after yourselves?
See you in a few years?

Who knows now?
Those conversations took off
with the wind over Llanafan
and never came back.

Someone might remember
the accident
with the steam engine
the cheap foreign lead
the drift to the cities
the cough.

But that's not enough for me.
I want to lean on that gate
look in your eyes and ask
what took you away?

What longing in your poet soul
sent you wandering?
Was strong enough
to override your chapel interdictions
a life of lessons in duty
in provision
in fatherhood?

Or did the meetings merely aspirate your lungs
give service to your lips?

William Richards stonemason
they called you
so you would have known about building.
Did you never make the connection
between building and fatherhood
between abandonment and decay?

You left us letters and notebooks
full of poems brimming with guilt
that urged God's message to the needy
and gave surrogate succor
while the infants dwindled in their bowls
and in your prodigal conscience.

Leaving

We have all left
some clean some not so clean
some so strong
there is no justification
and we override the rules
and ride the consequences
down the rapids of remorse.

How many words does it take to heal?
How many years?
How many deaths?

And who returns?
A few to town, some into the hills
some never
with no glance back –
call it ruthless call it heartless
call it iron cold
they settle their land
and reap their honest corn.

How many moons does it take to forgive?
How much forgetting?
How many strikes of the plough?

1918

death was everywhere that year

death in the sick room
death in confinement
death in the trenches
death in the mines

it's a wonder
the living
did not die of grief

Bargoed, 1921

What happened, Grandpa?
One day you filled
the busy valley church
with your stormy words
and your love of God
the next
you're visiting the sick
in Ysceifiog
just seven hundred souls
since so few came back
from Ypres and Gallipoli.

The question made my mother
repeat a grief-engraved surmise
though why should she remember?
She would best forget
keep walking to school
up the coal-black streets
forget her mother on her deathbed
forget her sister Gwladys
forget her brother Tom the TB took
forget the ailing infant Alwyn.

How much death can a young girl take
without some forgetting?
How much death can a strong man take
without a little help from the bottle?

I know what they're saying.
That he's close enough to his housekeeper
for a bit of comfort –
and so soon after his wife!
It's not becoming for a man of the cloth
an example to his parishioners.
And what about the girl –
the one that's left
the brainy one –
what will happen to her?

Dust muffles the voices
though there may be a vault
and a leather ledger
in a fine italic hand
with a list of his faults and his errors
the reasons why
it's better for all concerned.

The lord is my shepherd.
He leads his flock from field to field
opening and closing
the gates of his infinite pastures.
His plan unfolds from day to day
and he alone assumes the coat
from which our cloth is cut.

Tsientsin, 1935

Megan Myfanwy he called me.
He's a nice man
tall, and handsome too.
English, mind
but they're all right –
one at a time.

I don't know where he heard Myfanwy.
They introduced me as Megan.
But he pronounced it right
which is something –
shows he did his homework.

I think he'd be a good provider.
But what am I saying?
I've only met him twice.

I don't meet many people –
more than in Ysceifiog, mind you.
I take games after school
then there's papers to mark.

Funny really
him out here for business
me here teaching –
different, but not so different
when you think about it.
We're both just here
doing what we can.

So many White Russians!
Two girls in my class –
lost everything.
Nothing to go home to now –
not like us
though tad's not well
so soon there'll
only be Elvan –
and me.

Come Stranger

Come stranger
sing for me
in your voice
I hear
the sound of unasked questions
that stir my longing

Come wistful stranger
sing for me
in your eyes
I smell
the smoke of ancient hearths
where stories linger

Come dark-haired stranger
sing for me
in your face
I see
the look of love abandoned
the rue of intimacy

I too at home
long for home
with my man
long for a man
with my child
long for a child

Come stranger
sing me deep
sing me the story
sing me the heart of it

Cilcain, 1947

A letter came this morning
from Australia.
The cousins were displayed
before a flat horizon
in their short pants.

And here the cows amble home
between the hedgerows
udders swaying
and pause to look at me
bringing me
to a view of myself
standing
in the small of the lane
with my hand on the gate
as I have stood for centuries
in my leather boots
slapping the same warm hides
calling the same humble dogs
into the yard.

Not that I could ever leave
these fields and valleys –
(no, not could, for I could
but would, for I would not) –
the pull of somewhere else
for me the proof of God
this smallholding the proving ground
this land the blessing.

So I leave the gate
and follow the herd into the barn
to the warm milk smell
and the pails clanging
on the cobbles.

Plas Newydd, 1951

What have these grey stones
to do with me?

these barns
these heavy cows
this clattering yard
these dusty trophies
from the county show

this strong woman
in her milky headscarf
and dung-spattered boots

this dog-loved man
whiskered and tobacco-stained
a string around his coat

these fields
these staring sheep
this cloud-raced land
these sedges sodden
from the windswept rain

What have these Welsh hills
to do with me?

Hong Kong, 1952

All I can think now
is that they tried
to keep me from the confusion
of a Welsh mind trapped
in an English body.

Perhaps they knew
what I didn't then
that this particular complaint
needs for its expression
the sight of daffodils
the sound of Welsh voices
the fire of Cwm Rhondda
and theirs was an innocent attempt
to shelter me from my birthright.

Friday leaving for school
mother was at the dining room table
laying out the wire and the glue
and the crepe paper.
Later, walking up the drive
I could hear the Welsh ladies
on the front porch
giggling their goodbyes.

Saturday St. David's Day
I looked through the window
and watched my family
get into the car
and drive away.

Sunday at breakfast
in the paper
a photo of my sister
and her friend Rhiannon
looking pretty in their aprons
and black Welsh hats
greeting the photographer
with trays of daffodils
for his buttonhole.

Better eat my cornflakes
and pretend I don't care –
that this is just for girls
that being Welsh is about
dressing up
and making paper daffodils.

London, 1956

Meet me at the Welsh Club at four
she would say
and I did
skipping the steaming pavements
a hundred miles
between the arrival of the 7:42
to Waterloo
and the fireside cup of tea
and biscuits.

The Science Museum
a ride in the lift
to the Derry and Toms roof garden
lunch at Slaters
for half a crown
the Round Pond
the Serpentine
the final sprint
down Oxford Street.

So much to tell.

The song said
Maybe It's Because I'm A Londoner –
but I wasn't.

Guildford, 1962

Do you remember me?
You looked up and saw me
in the helicopter
at 500 feet
on my way to an accident on the A3.
I saw you, saw you clearly
shielding your eyes from the sun
saw your face even –
my shadow passed right over you –
saw your brown bag on the grass
like a body.
You were wearing a blue shirt.
You were on your own.
You were young and skinny.
Funny how clear things are from the air.
Got me thinking about freedom.
Youth and freedom came up a lot
in my profession.
Somewhere near Ripley
I heard the victim had died
so I circled round and
by the time I got back
you'd gone.
It was only ten minutes.
I went home after that.
My shift was up.
You have no idea
how that image sticks with me
how I've thought about you
over the years.

My wife had just left me
and there you were taking off
without a care in the world
your future beside you
on the grass.
It was early.
Did you wake in the field right there?
How far did you go that day?
And how strange these things are but
I could tell
that it was not escape
from the prison of your childhood
or a necessary journey from A to B
but just a whim
and a need to fulfill it –
nor did your map
have a place called future
or a sea called adventure
just roads and roundabouts
with here and there
a ferry to board
a mountain to climb
an ocean to cross.
How I envied you!
Now I sit in my wheelchair
and watch the sycamore
by the shed
spin its seeds
to earth.

Rhydymwyn, 1975

He showed me his notebook of hymn tunes
and sang one through in Welsh.
The hearth smelled of permanence
the polish had heard it before
and his son my cousin my face my closest blood
next to me with his cardigan and his silent wife
in the circumscription of their contentment
was as far from me as Pant y Hirion.

As if my father's line
had oiled the water of my ancestry
and rendered it distasteful.
The added inches bought from England
at a price I never settled on
disguised my origins and made them stranger to me
the extra adding stature only in my exile
but diminution at my roots.

But why complain? – for I was gone by then
not just from those bald mountains
or to Dover and beyond to these wild woods
but to another planet with no way back
to embrace the doilies of Rhydymwyn
and understand what they were talking about
or jump off the back of a Number 9 bus
onto the fields of Ceredigion.

St. Albans, 1984

something was troubling her at the end
alone in her English flat
with her occasional English friends
visited by her English children
and their English children
the line broken
the language an abandoned vehicle
mention of Wales
more a joke
or a slap on the back
on St. David's Day
than the buzz of belonging
family dead or scattered
last heard of
smudged and barely legible
in a small brown book
at a sheep station in Queensland
the remaining drops of this distillate
dispersed
on an island of indifference
with no way left to reach the mainland
though they take time off
from tennis and golf
to watch the highlights
of the National Eisteddfod

Roots

Roots roots so many roots
Roots roots under your boots
Carrots potatoes turnips and beets
Solid and filling not wimpy like fruits.

Roots roots how do you trace 'em?
That's not a problem but can you embrace 'em?
Thank heavens that's something I'll never do.
Don't be so certain – we all have to face 'em.

Roots roots deep in the soil
Soon to be lifted and wrapped up in foil.
Pull 'em up tear 'em up any old way
Dig for a while and you'll turn up a royal.

Roots roots where do I look?
Go to the library pick up a book.
That's very easy for you to say
But what if I find a tart or a crook?

Roots roots so many recipes
Mash 'em with butter whip 'em with cheese
Boil 'em in water fry 'em in oil
Mix 'em with mushrooms do as you please.

Roots roots digging for dirt
He was a con man she was a flirt.
Never have to be stodgy and bland
Add sugar and cinnamon make a dessert.

Roots roots over the sea
Dig 'em and cook 'em and have 'em for tea.
Tell 'em I'm hungry and make lots and lots
And swear cross your heart that you'll leave some for me.

Returning

The photo on the card said Tal-y-Llyn, and there
outside a post office on a main street sidewalk
I was surrounded by words I never learned in class –
mailbox, parking lot, stop light, trash –

and the cut of the clothes of the people walking by
the way they crossed the street to park their cars
the short hard shadows, a distant police car siren
struck me now as coarse, unwelcoming and foreign.

Outside a shop I was approached with a petition
bright faces sure of their consumer rights
and played my alien card to smile and turn away
not quite my problem I was glad to say.

Perhaps I'd always felt the tremor of displacement
a sideways glance of exile, checking for the charge
of infidelity from my corner of fugitive disgrace
a lack of native ease – my father's place, his father's place.

Inside the bank I joined a lunchtime queue
and took the card again and saw the quiet lake
a steam train puffing past the rowan and the oak
heard the whistle, smelled the smoke.

And it seemed as if the certainty of place had slipped
and left behind a dining room in Towyn
a wide bay window looking out across the sea
my mother charming guests for word games after tea

leaving me to ask again the question
of loyalty to here or there
recipient of drafts and statements overseas
shuffling forward in the line – Next customer please.

Now on another pavement a jet-lag day away
I wait for a bus the timetable flapping
my corner of the shelter cold and dank
beside the flaking stonework of a high street bank.

A girl with a child in a pushchair stands on her own
stares at her feet takes out her phone
and I see from her speech and her complexion
that I've left it too late to make the connection.

And the realization slowly dawns
that I've just given up the mediocrity of exile –
ravished by the ecstasy of earth –
without a chance to claim the genius of birth.

The story of there lies exposed as a myth
for I am entirely here. How cold the April wind!
How pink the phone that she is texting with!
How young, how white, how pierced her skin!

Eisteddfod

Like the cricket
or the grasshopper warbler
ecstatic in its thrall
our music permeates all
no source or direction
or quest for perfection
so shall we sing
kin with every singing thing
one heart one blood
our voice a flood
that fills the space
as our embrace
and proves we need no amplification
or instantaneous translation
to spread the sound to hidden places
touch and light a thousand faces

Aberystwyth, 2012

Are these the people?

These rugged brute-faced men
rugby players
laughing into their lagers.

Are these the people?

These creamy diaphanous girls
caring not a jot
baring their arms to the wind.

Are these the people?

These tiny women arm in arm
bent with gossip
buoyed by the bubbles of Welsh.

Gathering

I'm not quite sure what I'm doing here
To tell you the truth
How I should sit and present myself.
It is not natural to be invited like this.

Tell us something about yourself, you said
Your problems, your fears
Your struggles to make ends meet.
It can be hard, I know

To fulfil your duty to your family
While a deep voice says
Tell the world *I am here*
This is the mark I make.

That's what you said, but
We're not used to the spotlight.
We do our job, what God has given us.
Yes, I'll have a cup of tea, thank you.

Waiting, now, looking out of the window.
I think it's clearing from the west.
Should be dry for the walk home
over the hill to Plas Newydd.

It's been five years now since Delyth left.
Don't know how I've survived.
Lynn's there, in Cardiff, with the children
and Dave of course.

They come up now and then.
It's hard to get away these days.

I liked Elvan's hymn.
He still has a voice.
And William's poems
Fancy writing those from so far away!
Megan is such a flirt
Always was.
Still likes the men
Always did.
Was she happy?
You mean, because she left?
I don't know.
No happier than the rest of us.

Me? My turn?
All right, then.
Well, I thought I'd give you a little recitation.
It can be in English, right?
OK then. Here we go.

Mother would shoot out snippets of Welsh and watch, sideways, hoping for a glimmer of recognition, a brightening of interest, a sign of ancient cells stirring, but I turned away to my book of trains. It was hidden too deep, held in the convoluted coils of immaturity, biding its time, not knowing how long it would wait or even what it was waiting for. When I started exploring on my own I got shot at cycling over the mountains from Rhayader with my panier bags. *Don't come and steal our language,* they said, *Like you've stolen everything else.* Well, I never stole anything, but I didn't want to cause any trouble. Who was I to know what all that was about? I was only fourteen. So I backed off. Cycled like mad down the road, of course, back of my neck prickling. Slept in a few barns. Climbed Cader Idris. Went back to England. Put Wales behind me for another day. I was always *them*, you see, never *us*. That was the problem.

Last Poem

I had expected to end
this suite of reflections
of movements played
between the New World and the Old
with something strong and worthy
a dazzling coda
with a final blazing chord
to bring you to your feet
or a parting gift –
clarity in a silk-lined box
tied with a bow
and a card with your name on it.

This to provide some insight
a little closure, comfort
compensation for attention
not otherwise acknowledged.

But the metaphor collapses –
insight is blinded by brilliance
clarity may not lead to comfort
and closure is the goal of grieving –
though compensation's always nice
for otherwise who cares?
What keeps us marching
down these land-mined roads?
What is the spark that
fires our acts?

Is it hope or a dream
or a centripetal ache

requiring attention
or restlessness
a lovesick homesick who knows what
a craving of our pregnancy with God
a longing that we stuff
as soon as it appears
with rituals love affairs
and trips to the Bahamas
or psychoactive substances?

Though still it asks for more
our great black hole
the ultimate renewable
source of perpetual motion
to get us up and out
away from our incestuous ties
to foolproof couplings
that evolution demands.

And while it has a monstrous appetite
the wise say better not to throw it
every bone that comes our way –
excursions desertions conversions
are trifles that merely make it twitch its tail.

We've always suspected what would satisfy it
so when we've thrown it all we own
we can start to feed it what we don't
the transitory hopes and dreams
which have defined and scattered us

and sacrifice our darlings and our fears
our search for an external prize
the castles and bodies of beyond us
that will drop us on a windswept pavement
exhausted by our life's adventures
enlightened yes by what we've lost
but lightened more by what we've gained.

About the Author

Tony Kendrew went to school in England, where his early attempts at writing were full of mountains, rivers, birds and flowers.

He traveled widely before moving to the States in the early eighties and now lives and writes in Northern California, surrounded by imagery for his continuing love affair with nature. This usually finds its way into his poems, together with the big question he likes to address:

What on earth are we doing here?

Tony started reading his work at writers' groups and locally at cafés and gatherings in the nineties, and published a collection of his poems on CD in 2009 titled *Beasts and Beloveds*. Later that year he was invited to read at the Walking Words Festival in Telluride, Colorado, where he also took part in the Poetry in the Schools program at Telluride Middle School.

Tony has a degree from Cambridge University and a further degree and teaching credential from the University of London. In 2012 he began a year at the University of Wales doing a Masters Degree in Creative Writing. While in Wales he had a poem published in the collection *Poetry from Strata Florida*, and was invited to present his poems at Writers' Day at the Dylan Thomas Centre in Swansea. His MA dissertation became the current volume, *Turning*, and his first collection of poems *Feathers Scattered in the Wind* was published by Iconau in 2014.

You are invited to contact the poet via this book's website, www.turningpoems.com, where you can also find audio recordings of readings of some of the poems, and a link to a short video of the poem *Pant y Hirion, 1876*. The mailing address is 4751 Feliz Creek Road, Hopland, CA 95449, USA.

The *Turning* poems are also available as a CD, read by the poet.

Printed in Great Britain
by Amazon